FREE,
PERFECT
AND NOW

A LEAN SIX SIGMA
MONEY BELT MANIFESTO

JAY ARTHUR

Upgrade Your KnowWare!

Published by KnowWare International Inc.
2253 S. Oneida St. Ste 3D
Denver, CO 80224
(888) 468-1537
knowwareman@qimacros.com
www.qimacros.com

ISBN 978-1-884180-59-0

Publisher's Cataloging-in-Publication Data
Arthur, Jay
   Free, Perfect and Now / by Jay Arthur
      p.   cm.
   Includes bibliographical references.
   ISBN 978-1-884180-59-0
   1. Business
   2. Quality

HF5549.5M63A47   2011
658.3'14–DC20   00-193560 CIP

Printed in the United States of America
10 9 8 7 6 5 4 3 2 1

Table of Contents

The #1 question people ask when considering Lean Six Sigma is:

"Is it worth it?"

By which they mean:

Can I afford a long, drawn out, complicated change to my work life in a crazy-busy, overworked world where I don't want to add one more thing to my "to do" list? And will Lean Six Sigma deliver immediate, bottom-line, profit-enhancing, career-building results?

This manifesto answers these questions.

If you don't have the time to read the whole manifesto, here's what it says:

Whether you are a mom-and-pop store or a Fortune 500 company, to get the U.S. economy, your business, and your life back on track, you are going to want to start plugging the leaks in your cash flow. The solution to seemingly complex business problems is surprisingly simple and implementable.

I helped a hospital system start saving $5,000,000 a year in less than five days. I helped a cell phone company start saving $3,000,000 a year in five days. And I helped a muffler shop simplify, streamline and optimize daily operations to compete with a nearby chain store. I use Lean Six Sigma in my business to deliver fast, affordable, flawless Lean Six Sigma methods and tools.

Lean Six Sigma, as it is traditionally implemented, takes too long, costs too much and often fails to deliver the results expected. You can't afford to spend a fortune training "belts" on all of the methods and tools in the hopes that they will find and plug the leaks in your cash flow. You can't afford to wait months or years for results.

Instead, the future belongs to companies whose "Money Belts" can use the "Magnificent Seven" tools to maximize profits while minimizing costs. Money Belts can be trained in a day and start delivering results in five days or less.

Is Lean Six Sigma For You?

- Do you have too much fire fighting and crisis management?

- Is there too much rework and repair of error-prone products and services?
- Do you have too many angry customers?
- Are you losing business to faster, better and cheaper competitors?

Questions This Manifesto Answers:

1. Why is it foolish to spend a fortune training lots of Green and Black Belts on every tool and then start lots of teams?

2. Why do half of all Six Sigma implementations fail?

3. Why is all of the folklore about implementing Lean Six Sigma totally wrong minded?

4. What are the key tools you need to solve 99% of all business problems and maximize results?

5. How can every business, large or small, service or manufacturing, government or public sector use Lean Six Sigma to achieve breakthroughs in speed, quality and profitability?

Yes, this book is short, because if it's short, it's more likely to be read and used. I believe that you don't need to know everything about Lean Six Sigma to start getting results. Unless you work on a factory floor making complicated stuff like jet engines, there's a limit to how much is useful to learn.

So, you won't need to learn the hundreds of tools in the Lean Six Sigma body of knowledge. You will learn about the "Magnificent Seven" tools that will change your life, your business and create an unstoppable economy. It's possible to start using the tools of Lean Six Sigma immediately to get results without spending a fortune.

My Contrarian View

They say we need Green Belts and Black Belts.

I say we need Money Belts.

They say we need training to get results.

I say we need results; learning is a by-product.

They say it takes 5-10-20 days of training to be a belt.

I say you can learn to be a Money Belt in a day.

They say you need to know statistics.

I say your software should know statistics; you should know how to interpret them.

They say Lean Six Sigma takes a long time.

I say you can start getting results immediately.

They say you need complex, expensive software to do Six Sigma.

I say you need the affordable QI Macros for Excel.

They say Lean Six Sigma inhibits innovation.

I say it reveals opportunities for innovation and enhances it.

They say my approach to Lean Six Sigma is too simplistic.

I say I'm a realist about today's crazy-busy, do-more-with-less global business environment.

My Story

In the early 1990s I lived through a typical Six Sigma implementation at US West, one of the Baby Bells. We trained lots of belts and started lots of teams. But at the end of a year, only three out of a hundred teams had finished a project and delivered results. Pretty pathetic.

But I also noticed that the three successful teams did their next project in 3 months or less. The next in three weeks and ultimately they all got down to three days.

I wondered: Why not skip the "learning curve" and start solving problems in 3-to-5 days?

So I analyzed what made teams fail and what made them successful. Then I designed the Lean Six Sigma Money Belt system to make teams successful in a matter of days not months. I don't want you to waste time and money on Lean Six Sigma. I want you to start getting results right away.

Traditional Lean Six Sigma implementations *begin with training*, 5-10-20 days of training spanning several weeks or months. Then you start teams that span weeks or months and hope that somehow bottom-line, profit and productivity enhancing results will come out of the process. Sometimes they do; most of the time they don't.

I remember telling my boss that quality was about getting better, faster and cheaper. In typical Bell System fashion, he told me that I could have any two of the three: better and faster, but not cheaper; faster and cheaper, but not better; or better and cheaper, but not faster. Sadly, in 1995, after five years, the leadership team shut down the quality department. Five years later, Qwest bought US West and in 18 months the stock went from $60 to $1 per share.

Free, Perfect and Now

Don't let this happen to you! Don't let any-two-of-the-three thinking bring your company to its knees. I no longer say that quality is about getting better, faster and cheaper, because the paradigm has changed. Google has taught people that you can get whatever you want free, perfect and now! It's no longer good enough to be better, faster and cheaper; a company now needs to deliver products and services as close to free, perfect and now as possible.

I remember when I used to go to a brick-and-mortar bookstore to buy a book. If they didn't have it in stock, they would order it for me and I'd wait a week for delivery. Then Amazon made it possible to order the book on-line (now) and have it delivered overnight if necessary (now). Then the book industry took a huge leap toward now: you can download any eBook to a Kindle, Nook, or iPad immediately and pay less than you would for a printed copy of the book (cheaper, but not quite free).

Amazon understood America's obsession with *now* (saving time). Amazon and publishers understand that they can make as much money selling an eBook at a lower cost than they can if they print, store and ship a physical book. EBooks eclipsed the sales of physical books in May, 2011.

Some rock groups give their music away free to build an audience and then cash in by selling tickets and memorabilia at concerts.

Internet bandwidth doubles in speed and halves in cost every nine months. As Chris Anderson, author of *Free*, says: "When something halves in price each year, zero is inevitable!"

Now most people will say: "But everything can't be free!" True, but I say the new standard every business will be judged by is how close they can get to free, perfect and now. Companies need fast, affordable and flawless execution to deliver on the new market paradigm.

Unfortunately, the old trial-and-error, gut-feel approaches to improving performance are too slow and error-prone to deliver anything close to free, perfect and now. The only hope any business has is to adopt the methods and tools of Lean Six Sigma to simplify, streamline and optimize performance. Lean Six Sigma will not fix a company's inability to innovate, but it will ensure that any innovation is delivered in a fast, affordable and flawless manner.

Consumers have changed. Customers are smarter than most businesses. They quickly figure out which restaurants, retail shops, plumbers or whatever are fast, affordable and flawless, and social media like Facebook let's them tell everyone instantly. Critical care centers have sprung up because hospital emergency departments, in spite of their name, are too slow, averaging four hours for each patient, according to Press Ganey. This statistic has not changed for a decade. It's not that some hospitals aren't doing it faster and a lot better with better outcomes for patients; it's just that most aren't.

Most service businesses haven't explored Lean Six Sigma because they think it only applies to manufacturing. Information technologies departments haven't explored it because they don't think it applies to their software artisans. Of course, this is just lazy humans hoping the storm of free, perfect and now will pass them by.

Federal, state and local governments are struggling with budget deficits, but few have started using Lean Six Sigma to cut costs by 40%.

Lean Six Sigma can be applied anywhere to any business process. Anytime anything is produced or delivered, from a haircut to a congressional bill to a jet engine, it's because people follow a process. It may be a fast, affordable, flawless process or a sluggish, error-prone, costly one, but it's still a process. And Lean Six Sigma will simplify, streamline and optimize any process.

Unfortunately, Lean Six Sigma has its own problems. People think it costs too much and takes too long. Based on how most people implement it, this is no surprise, but we'll talk about that later. Over half the time, it fails to put down roots or is plucked like a weed by a new CEO or leadership team.

I say that Lean Six Sigma can be fast, affordable and flawless, maximizing results while minimizing costs. To do so requires a fresh approach using just a handful of tools to solve most of the problems facing businesses today. Training doesn't have to take weeks or months; it can be done in a matter of hours. Projects don't have to take weeks or months to complete; I've completed million dollar projects in five days or less. The actual analysis can be done quickly, but sometimes implementation can take longer because it has to go through some sluggish, error-prone process (IT for example).

Now some people will ask why everyone seems to be using the traditional, long, drawn out Lean Six Sigma implementation approach? Are they all wrong? I say, not all, but most are headed for disappointment. They will spend a lot of time and money training a lot of multicolored "belts," start teams that flounder and wonder what went wrong. Don't let this happen to you.

About once a week I get a call or email from someone who has read my Lean Six Sigma Demystified book. They invariably say: "I wish I'd read your book two years ago."

There is a better way, but you have to be willing to ease into it rather than jump into it. You have to be willing to narrow your focus, because performance problems aren't spread evenly over a company like butter on bread; they cluster in a few activities and gaps. To narrow your focus, you have to be willing to reduce the number of people involved. That's right, to accelerate adoption of Lean Six Sigma and increase results, you have to reduce the number of people involved.

No one needs yet another jargon-ridden, statistical recipe book on how to bake Lean Six Sigma into a corporate culture. It doesn't work because cultures aren't cakes. Cultures are more like a herd of bison or a school of fish always moving and shifting, sometimes slowly, sometimes quickly. We need a way to nudge the culture toward excellence that doesn't invite a charge from the bulls or trigger a stampede.

Companies don't need more Green Belts or Black Belts. They need Money Belts—people who can quickly find ways to save time and money to boost productivity and profitability. They have to learn how to eliminate the three silent killers of productivity and profitability: delay, defects and deviation. When they eliminate the delays, it makes the product or service available *now*. When they eliminate defects and deviation, products and services become *perfect*. Eliminating defects and deviation reduces costs so that products and services become more affordable, effectively *free*.

Wanted: Problem Solvers for Perilous Times

My goal is to create 100 million Money Belts dedicated to getting the world economy back on track. Change your life, your business and the world; be a Money Belt!

For employees who want to be indispensable over the next 10-20-30 years, learn the Magnificent Seven Tools of Lean Six Sigma. Use them to solve seemingly impossible problems, implement and sustain the solutions, and then keep going.

This is my Lean Six Sigma Money Belt Manifesto. Eliminate the three silent killers of productivity and profitability, and your business will experience a quantum leap toward *free*, *perfect* and *now*. To do so you don't need long, expensive training or endless team meetings. You need Money Belts focused on the most critical problems using the Magnificent Seven methods and tools to start getting results immediately. And it won't take long for customers to notice the improvement.

Jay Arthur
Denver, CO
September 2011

Top 10 Ways You Know You Need Lean Six Sigma

1. **Heroic efforts** are routinely required to prevent delivering a bad product or service creating a culture rewarding heroism.

2. **Customer complaints.** For every customer who complains about your product, there are 16 more that won't tell you directly. Each of these tells eight other people.

3. **Supplier complaints.** Do your suppliers complain about the irrational last minute demands you make and how long it takes to get paid?

4. **Employee whining:** "I can't do my job because..." Employees want to do a good job. What's stopping them?

5. **Blaming people, not processes**. 99% of the problems are caused by processes, not your people.

6. **Knee jerk fixes that fail.** Common sense and gut feel stop working at a 3-sigma (6% defects) level.

7. **Margins are low, expenses are high, growth is stalled.** Delay, defects and deviation inflate expenses and eat profits.

8. **Failures in the field.** How big is your warranty or repair department? How many people does it take to handle your customer service and tech support calls?

9. **Too many inspectors** checking quality. You can't inspect quality into your product or service, but you can build it in.

10. **Absenteeism and turnover.** Employees hate doing a poor job for customers. They get angry when the internal system prevents them from doing a good job. How are systems preventing your employees from doing a good job?

Chapter 1

Money Belt Manifesto

I just returned from working with a metal manufacturer grossing $200 million a year. They had been using Lean, but not Six Sigma. Why just Lean and not Six Sigma, you might ask?

Like many other companies, they thought Six Sigma would take too long, cost too much and fail to deliver results. Sadly, for most Six Sigma implementations, this is true. It's one of the reasons so many Six Sigma implementations fail in the first three years.

The Holy Grail for anyone who runs a company, either service or manufacturing, is fast, affordable, flawless execution that results in higher productivity, profitability and customer satisfaction.

Flawed execution is costly in time, money and customers. Flawless execution is priceless to you and your customer.

We live in a world where employees actively resist change, not because they are bad employees, but because they are too overwhelmed to do anything else. So it's imperative to stop trying to change them and, instead, create an environment where they participate in changing the process to achieve flawless execution.

Lean Six Sigma Can Be Fast and Affordable

I worked with the metal manufacturing company's leadership team for just three days. The first day, we focused on learning the essential methods and tools of Six Sigma using my QI Macros software for Excel. In the afternoon, we started analyzing data about defects such as inclusions in the finished product. The next day teams dove into solving key production and delivery problems.

After just a few hours using the QI Macros with my bare-bones, laser-focused Lean Six Sigma process, they had developed three killer improvement projects revolving around cycle time and defects. The only thing left to do was implement the changes and measure results.

If you have tools like the QI Macros and some data about delay, defects and deviation, it's easy to find the "invisible low hanging fruit" in any business.

The Three Silent Killers of Productivity and Profitability

Ask any business owner or executive, they know that something is killing productivity and profits, but that it is hard to put a finger on the culprit. While many people look for *someone* to blame, the problem is rarely a person. Invariably it's the *process*.

In any business, there are three silent killers of productivity and profitability: Delay, Defects and Deviation.

Delays: Most business processes grow up in an ad-hoc fashion over time. They have too many workarounds and rework loops. They suffer from too many unnecessary delays between steps.

Delays *are killing your productivity and profitability.*

Defects: Like it or not, every process produces defects. Even a profitable business can suffer from a 6% error rate across sales, marketing, ordering, fulfillment, invoicing, etc. **These defects cost a typical business one-third of total revenues.**

Defects *are killing your productivity and profitability.*

Deviation: Some products are a little too big or too small, too long or short, too wide or narrow. Some customer service processes take too long or cost too much. These are all forms of deviation (i.e., variation from a customer's ideal target value). Deviation results in recalls, returns, scrap, waste and rework that devour profits.

Deviation *is killing your productivity and profitability.*

Simple tools like control charts, pareto charts and histograms can diagnose problems with defects and deviation. SWAT (special weapons and tactics) teams of employees can quickly identify the root causes of problems and then implement countermeasures.

Once these problems are solved, productivity and profitability begin to flow easily from your business. It plugs the leaks in your cash flow. And, best of all, it helps to distinguish your company in the marketplace. Customers appreciate fast, affordable, flawless services and products, and they will tell their friends.

Most people think that problems are spread evenly all over the business. They are wrong. **You don't have to fix everything in your business.** And you don't have to fix them all at the same time. To maximize results and minimize costs, you only have to pinpoint the few key places that cause most of the delay, defects and deviation that cause lost profit and productivity.

Haven't you waited long enough to start eliminating the three silent killers that cause so much firefighting, crisis management, overtime, lost customers and sleepless nights? Isn't it time to start plugging the leaks in your cash flow? Or are you going to wait for one of your competitors to develop an unbeatable lead?

Your Fix-It Factory

Every company has two factories and I use the word "factory" loosely. It's not about manufacturing. It applies to any business process, service or manufacturing:

- One factory creates and delivers your product or service.

- The other, hidden "Fix-it Factory" cleans up all of the mistakes and errors that occur in the main factory. It employs up to a third of your staff.

If you're a 3-Sigma company (a six-percent error rate) and most companies are no better than 3-Sigma, the Fix-it Factory is costing you $25-40 of every $100 you spend.

If you're a $1 million company, that's $250,000-$400,000. In a $10 million company, that's $2.5-$4 million that you can add back into your bottom line. If you're a $100 million company, that's $25-40 million. If you're a $1 billion company, that's $250-$400 million. Just think what saving a fraction of that money could do for your productivity and profitability! And you only need a few methods and tools to get started with Lean Six Sigma.

Learn to FISH

The secret to Lean Six Sigma is learning how to use performance measurements to FISH—Focus, Improve, Sustain and Honor:

Focus: Laser-focus the improvement effort on the "vital few" problems that are killing your productivity and profitability. You don't need to fix everything, just the vital few. There are hidden gold mines in your business, but you will need the tools of Lean Six Sigma to find them!

Laser focus only requires seven key methods and tools. You can learn these methods and tools in a matter of hours at: www.lean-six-sigma-money-belt.com.

Improve: Analyze the root causes and make improvements that will systematically cut costs and boost profits by $25 or more out of every $100 you spend.

To eliminate unnecessary delays, you only need Post-it® Notes. To reduce or eliminate defects and deviation you will need control charts, pareto charts and histograms. These are easily created in Microsoft Excel using the QI Macros (www.qimacros.com/excel-spc-software.html).

Sustain: Use control charts to monitor and maintain the new level of improvements, because otherwise you'll fall back into old habits and lower levels of performance.

Honor: Honor your progress. Recognize and reward improvements. Refocus and start on a new problem or issue.

I can hear some of you whining: "I don't have time to learn new methods and tools." To which I say: "If you want the benefits, you only have to learn a few key tools, not everything under the sun."

The Long Tail of Tools

Most Lean Six Sigma training covers what I call the "long tail" of improvement methods and tools. It includes every tool you might ever need if you work on a manufacturing factory floor. And it's not that these tools aren't useful in certain situations, but the Magnificent Seven will solve 99 percent of the problems facing most businesses. The rest are overkill when starting the journey from 3-to-6 sigma. And Black Belts freely admit that when faced with a more complex problem, they often have to look up what to do because they've forgotten everything from their training.

In the U.S., only one person out of 100 works on a manufacturing plant assembly line. These employees need the "long tail" of methods and tools.

The other 99% of people work in services, sales, marketing, purchasing, accounting, and so on. They only need the right methods and tools used in the right order to start finding and fixing problems that consume a third or more of total revenues. These are the people who can most benefit from becoming a Money Belt.

My advice? Master the "Magnificent Seven" tools that will solve most problems, then add in the tools from the long tail, as needed, either through training, reading a book or on-line resource.

You can move rapidly from 3-sigma to 6-sigma using only maps of process flow, a few key problem solving tools (control chart, pareto chart, histogram and root cause analysis), and control charts to monitor and sustain the improvements.

So, why do companies, both big and small, spend so much money training Six Sigma belts in all of the exotic tools of Six Sigma when most of the bang-for-the-buck comes from just these few simple tools? Beats me! It must be a common management delusion that complexity delivers value. What companies need are Money Belts!

Why Am I Ranting About Money Belts?

If you have sluggish, error-prone processes that irritate customers and employees, and consume a third of your revenues, you can't afford to ignore these tools.

Most companies cannot afford to spend months or years implementing Lean Six Sigma. And most people can't afford the time or money to attend the 5-10-20 day trainings. It's overkill. You can, however, learn the essential tools quickly and start using them immediately. It's as close to free, perfect and now as is humanly possible.

Are You A Lean Six Sigma Money Belt?

I've lived through a wall-to-wall, floor-to-ceiling implementation of Lean Six Sigma methods. I've made all of the mistakes and learned how to avoid them. The methods and tools are easy; getting people to want to use them is hard. So, I've had to find ways to make it as fast, affordable and flawless as possible.

From my perspective, there are too many people trained and certified as belts. Too many teams started. And not enough results. This causes at least half of Lean Six Sigma programs to die after about three years.

The hype, jargon and mass trainings normally associated with Lean Six Sigma aren't necessary to achieve dramatic, lasting improvements quickly.

In this Money Belt Manifesto:

- You won't learn everything in the Green Belt or Black Belt body of knowledge.

- You won't be "certified." Your certification is the projects you've worked on and how much money you've saved.

- You will only learn the methods and tools necessary to slay the three silent killers of productivity and profitability.

- You'll learn how to start plugging the leaks in your cash flow.

- You'll learn how to sustain improvements so that you don't backslide.

- You'll learn how to wrangle the dreamers, realists and critics in your leadership and improvement teams.

Why is Lean Six Sigma So Important?

1. It's a winner-take-all global economy. If you aren't willing to chase the dream of fast, affordable, flawless execution, someone else will. The early adopters achieve an unbeatable lead.

2. We waste too much time, money and resources fixing stuff that shouldn't be flawed.

3. The profit from plugging the leaks in your cash flow is huge—a third or more of total revenues.

4. The productivity that comes from plugging the leaks in your cash flow is huge—2X, 4X, even 8X improvements are possible.

5. Fast, affordable, flawless companies will create an unstoppable economy in those countries that jump on the Lean Six Sigma bandwagon.

Five Ways Lean Six Sigma Can Help You

1. When customers realize that they don't have to wait for your product or service they will tell everyone they know. And those people will beat a path to your door. This used to take a long time, but with Facebook and Twitter, it now happens in seconds.

2. When customers realize that there are no hidden costs for repairs, returns or other issues with your product or service, word of mouth and "word of mouse" will fill your store.

3. When your do-it-yourself product goes together effortlessly without missing parts or pieces, customers will love you.

4. When your restaurant customers get exactly what they ordered, quickly, with an accurate bill every time, they will encourage their friends to give you a try.

5. When your software and operating systems never crash, hang or stall, it will win your repeat business.

So, how can you do this? Use this book with the video training at www.lssmb.com. Every quick video of key methods and tools will be short—under 10 minutes. You can watch them over and over again as needed to learn the methods and tools.

There will be case studies you can download to test your skills.

You might be wondering, Jay why are you giving this video training away for free?

First, it's just not possible to train 99% of the world's population in Money Belt Skills even if I started today and trained 100s of trainers. But it is possible on-line.

Second, many people who want Lean Six Sigma training can't afford it. But they can afford Money Belt training because it's free. Or they can't afford the 1-4 weeks it takes to get the traditional training. And none can afford to spend 14 weeks solving a problem.

Third, Six Sigma requires software to analyze the data in ways that pinpoints where to make improvements. While I'm offering a free 90-day trial of the QI Macros software at www.qimacros.com/demystified.html, I hope everyone will buy a copy because they will need it to find and fix the problems that consume a third or more of total revenue. Then they will need it to monitor and maintain the improvement.

Fourth, if you like my message, you might consider inviting me to train and coach your organization. Or you might consider having us analyze some data to focus your initial improvement efforts. Or use our one-on-one consulting to jump start your efforts.

And, if nothing else, a faster, better, cheaper experience in every restaurant and business I do business with would make my time on this planet much more pleasant. I'm tired of being part of their Fix-It Factory. I end up doing too much inspection and rework that I shouldn't have to do.

When the Green Belt and Black Belt craze dies away, Money Belts who can help companies get closer to free, perfect and now will always be in demand.

Be a Money Belt!

Chapter Two
Free

It's as if our brains were wired to raise a flag every time we're confronted with a price. This is the "is it worth it?" flag. By charging a price, any price, creates a mental barrier that most people won't bother crossing. Free, in contrast, speeds right past that decision, increasing the number of people who will try something.. - Chris Anderson

Free? How can our product or service be free? You might think I'm out of my mind, but as Chris Anderson explains in his book *Free*, the costs of all things digital are falling to zero while power and performance are doubling every year or two. "This 'triple play' of faster, better, cheaper technologies—processing, storage and band-width—all come together on-line." Anderson says this is the paradox of free: "People are making lots of money charging nothing." He calls this new economic reality, *Freeconomics.*

In *Unleashing the Ideavirus*, Seth Godin wrote: "Twenty years ago, the top 100 companies in the Fortune 500 either dug something out of the ground or turned a natural resource into something you could hold." Today, only 32 do. Since only one person out of every hundred still works on a factory floor making a tangible product, that means that the rest of us are involved in intangible products (i.e., digital ones that can benefit from Freeconomics).

Digital products include orders, invoices, purchasing, payments, emails, websites, apps, eBooks, etc. Even in manufacturing, when a customer places an order for a product, the ordering and invoicing costs are basically free, paid for by the product. Got a customer service desk? Free. Why do companies provide "frequently asked questions" (FAQs) on their websites? Because it's free. Customers can take care of themselves. Get the idea? Every business provides lots of free services. The more you can drive these costs to zero, the better off you will be. Lean Six Sigma can help drive these costs to zero.

The Freemium Business Model

Anderson describes the path to making money with free as follows:

1. Build a community around free advice and information.

2. With the community's help, design products that people want.

3. Create a freemium version and a premium version that people pay for to save time and reduce the risks of a do-it-yourself version.

4. Build in a profit margin to cover the cost of free.

Why did I put up a free Lean Six Sigma Money Belt training on YouTube (www.lssmb.com)? Because training is the bottleneck that prevents mass adoption of Lean Six Sigma. Why would I want mass adoption? Because it's almost impossible to do Six Sigma without software to draw all of the charts and graphs. The training is free in hopes that more people will buy the QI Macros for Excel (www.qimacros.com).

How does Lean Six Sigma Play into Free?

Anderson says: People will pay to save time, lower risk and improve status. People will pay for things they love. FedEx will get your letter or box wherever you want it to go overnight. It costs more than sending it via mail, but the time saved makes the price of the service essentially free. The ability to do things faster than the competition makes a product or service essentially free.

If I want to make a phone call, I don't want to find a pay phone. Like billions of people over the last 20 years, I use my cell phone. Convenience is effectively *free*.

If I buy a product, I expect it to work right the first time. Working right the first time and every time afterward helps make the product free. If I plug it in and it doesn't work or doesn't work correctly, I then have to waste my precious time figuring out why and going back to the store I bought it from to return or repair the item. The delays, waste and rework involved make the product unbearably expensive. Your time is valuable and so is your customer's.

If I go to a restaurant and they get my order wrong, I have to wait for them to redo the order (unnecessary delay and waste). Why do people frequent fast-food restaurants? Because the food is dependable, predictable and delivered quickly.

Hint: Most fast food restaurants use Lean production cells with error-free methods for assembly. What can you learn from their success?

The cost of any product or service is not just the sticker price, but also the time and effort required to get it, use it and maintain it. Everyone is too busy to deal with even the slightest inconvenience. It's the nonmonetary costs that make things prohibitively expensive.

Lean can eliminate the delays and Six Sigma can eliminate the defects and deviation that add unnecessary costs to any product or service. Lean Six Sigma can make a product or service seem free.

Google handles two-thirds of the world's search traffic for free. Google makes money on ads placed around the search. 80% of people click on the free links. 20% click on paid links. Free worked for Google.

Robert Wood Johnson's Emergency Room implemented a 15-30 minute guarantee—patients would see a nurse in 15 minutes and a doctor in 30 minutes or their visit was free. Not surprisingly, when compared to the four hour waits in other emergency rooms, this was a form of free. The hospital's ER business grew by over 10% per year and had to add another wing onto the hospital to handle the load.

Here's the *New Reality:*

Now is free. Fast is free. Delayed is expensive.

Flawless is free. Defective is expensive.

Precision is free. Deviation is expensive.

All three are the killer app for making a product or service, even one you pay for, seem free. And Lean Six Sigma is the way to achieve breakthroughs in fast, flawless delivery that will make your products and services more affordable and desirable.

Chapter Three

Now!

Instant gratification takes too long. - Carrie Fisher

Nike's slogan is "Just Do It!" For businesses, the new slogan is "Just Do It NOW!" Customers no longer want to wait for anything if they know it's possible to get it right now. So every business has two choices: 1) figure out how to deliver the product or service immediately or 2) wait for someone else to figure out how to just do it now and put you out of business.

Fortunately, the Toyota Production System (a.k.a. Lean) has figured out how to simplify and streamline any business process to make it lightning fast. To just do it now, we have to reduce DOWNTIME:

- **D**elay – Unnecessary delays between steps in a process
- **O**verproduction – making stuff that no one has ordered

- **W**aste and Rework – caused by mistakes, errors, defects and deviation
- **N**on-value added processing (e.g., inspection and rework)
- **T**ransportation – unnecessary movement of materials
- **I**nventory – unnecessary raw materials, work in process or finished goods
- **M**otion – unnecessary movement of employees
- **E**mployee creativity – unused wisdom of the workers

While most manufacturing companies have figured out how to optimize the production line using these tools, they represent less than one percent of the American economy. The other 99 percent of companies are barely aware of how to simplify and streamline business operations. Based on my experience in all kinds of industries from healthcare to telecom to IT to manufacturing, a couple of key insights will slash the time it takes to do anything.

Delay

In most service businesses and the "back room" functions of all businesses, **unnecessary delays between steps are the main cause of sluggish performance**. Most business processes get more and more complex over time. Problems evolve into workarounds and rework loops. Problems lead to unnecessary delays between steps.

When most people look at a process, they see a flowchart that looks like this:

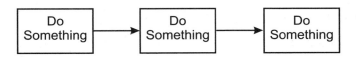

I see something very different, huge delays and piles of unfinished work products:

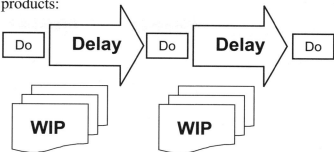

There's very little actual "doing" and a whole lot of delay (i.e., waiting around). And most businesses do things in big batches so that there is always work in process (WIP) laying around. Big batches supposedly create economies of scale, but all they do is create opportunities for mistakes, errors and additional delays.

This leads us to a few simple rules:

The 3-57 Rule: In most businesses, employees are only working on the product or service for 3 minutes out of every hour, leaving 57 minutes of delay. To this most managers will say: "But my people are busy!" Yes they are, but the thing going through the process isn't. It's idle 95 percent of the time—57 minutes per hour. Don't believe me? Start with any customer order and follow it around. Bring a novel to pass the time.

The Dark Side of the 3-57 Rule: Trying to make people faster is a waste of time, because employees only account for 3 minutes out of every 60. You have to make your lazy product faster by eliminating the delays between processing steps.

The 15-2-20 Rule: For every 15 minutes per hour you reduce those 57 minutes of delay, you will double productivity and increase profit margins by 20 percent. Since it's usually easy to eliminate these delays, it's possible to boost productivity two-four-eight fold and profit margins by 20-40-80-100 percent. With Lean tools it's easy to do this quickly.

The Dark Side of the 15-2-20 Rule: Every increase in delay decreases productivity and profitability. Example: approvals. Most companies have too many sign-offs and approvals when it comes to buying or doing anything. Result: unnecessary delay.

The 3x2 Rule: Reducing delays enables any business to grow three times faster than its competition and double productivity.

The Dark Side of the 3x2 Rule: If you don't get faster, your competitors will.

How do we achieve these breakthrough reductions in delay?

First, Simplify the Workspace

Any workspace collects clutter. The Lean "5S" process is like spring cleaning. Just get a small team to spend a few hours to:

- **Sort** the needed from the unneeded (e.g., outdated forms, unused machines and materials, etc.). Dispose of the unneeded stuff.
- **Straighten** by making everything visual and self-explanatory (e.g., color-code and label them).
- **Shine** – clean the workspace.
- **Standardize** the ongoing sorting, straightening and shining of the workspace.
- **Sustain** the simplification process by repeating every few months.

Once you've simplified the workspace using 5S, it's easy to redesign the workflow and workspace for optimal performance.

Then, Map the Value Stream

It's easy to eliminate delays. Simply flowchart or map the value stream. (Watch my video at www.lssmb.com/lean-value-stream-map-patient-scheduling.html or http://www.youtube.com/watch?v=3mcMwlgUFjU.)

Put times on each arrow of the process. You'll quickly discover that most of the cycle time is consumed *between* steps.

Redesign the process to eliminate delays. You should be able to eliminate 80-90 percent of the overall cycle time which will boost productivity and profits by 50 percent or more.

It only takes a handful of Post-it® Notes, a flipchart, a few workers and two-to-four hours to diagnose and redesign most processes for improved efficiency and effectiveness.

Then, Diagram the Movement of Employees and Work Products

Again, using Post-its and a flipchart, a handful of workers can diagram the workspace and movement of employees and materials through the space. If you're not sure how to do it, just follow a variety of customer orders around the office, factory, hospital or other facility. An aptly named "spaghetti diagram" will rise from this analysis.

Spaghetti Diagram Video: www.youtu.be/UmLrDjT5g8o

Simply rearrange processing "stations" to minimize movement of people and products.

Then, Shift from Economies of Scale to Economies of Speed

One of the secrets of Toyota's Production System is called one-piece flow. The idea is to get down to a batch size of one, not 100 or 1000. When you can make one of anything immediately, you don't need any inventory. If Taco Bell can take a drive-through order, make a taco and a burrito, take payment and deliver the order in 180 seconds, why can't you do the same thing with whatever it is that you do?

What if you don't make anything? Sure you do. Every office worker produces forms. Service reps produce orders. Computers produce transactions.

Simply redesign the process to reduce batch sizes, ideally to a size of one. An exception to this rule might occur when customers always order 100 a month. From a load-leveling perspective, it may be more efficient to produce 25 a week.

I worked with a company that printed national magazines. They printed a million at a time (big batch). But the bindery could only glue or staple 200,000 a day (smaller batch). The other 800,000 (overproduction) had to be stored somewhere (unnecessary movement of inventory), where they could be hit by passing forklifts (waste and rework). By switching to a quick changeover process, they could print 250,000 the first day and an additional 200,000 each subsequent day until they had met the volume required. This made it easier to schedule other, higher profit jobs in between runs. It eliminated unnecessary inventory and motion. And, if they discovered a printing error at the bindery (waste and rework), they didn't have to reprint the entire run.

I worked with a hospital lab. We had the lab techs wear pedometers for a week and record their travel distances. Techs were walking two-to-four miles a day (unnecessary motion) in the 2400 sq. ft. lab. By rearranging the machines in the lab, putting the highest volume ones into work cells, we were able to reduce movement by over 50 percent saving an estimated seven hours of delay per day, accelerating diagnosis, treatment and discharge of patients.

I worked with a computer operations group that couldn't get nightly batch processing done in time to bring up the on-line systems in the morning. They thought they were going to have to buy a new mainframe computer at a cost of several million dollars. After laying out the nightly process, we found 32 decision points where the process waited on a technician to verify and release the next job in the string. A new employee suggested that the computer's operating system could handle most of these checks (employee wisdom). By shifting 30 of the 32 decisions to the operating system, the nightly batch run fell from nine hours to just one (a 90% reduction).

These are the kinds of opportunities that exist in every business.

So there you have it, the essence of Lean. There's a lot more depth to be explored, but for most companies, delays are the number one problem. Once those are gone, you'll be ready for ways to refine the steps in the process. First, spend some time simplifying and streamlining the existing process. And there are added benefits.

Lean's Secret By-product

One of the lesser known by-products of simplifying and streamlining the process is a 50 percent reduction in defects. That's right! Lean will cut defect rates in half. When employees don't have to pick up where they left off, remember where they were, do something and set the product or service back down to wait for the next step in processing, when they can handle it using one-piece flow, they have no opportunity to make a mistake, miss a step or do a step twice. The chance of error falls dramatically.

Everyone's Secret Fear

Employees fear that Lean will eliminate jobs and it will...from the Fix-it Factory. What employees don't understand is that many more jobs will open up to serve all of the new and repeat customers.

People sometimes ask: "Jay, should I start with Lean or Six Sigma?" I say if delays are costing you customers, start with Lean. Defect reduction is a by-product. It doesn't take a lot of fancy tools or methods. The process is simple.

Lean: Simplify and Streamline the Process

1. 5S the workspace.

2. Map the Value Stream paying special attention to the delays between work activities.

3. Map unnecessary movement of people and products using a Spaghetti Diagram.

4. Redesign to eliminate the delays.

5. Redesign to eliminate unnecessary movement.

6. Redesign for one-piece flow.

7. Repeat until you can just do it now!

Chapter 4

Perfect

The mechanic that would perfect his work must first sharpen his tools. - Confucius

The 1960s film, *The Magnificent Seven*, starred Yul Brenner, Steve McQueen, Charles Bronson, James Coburn, Robert Vaughn, Brad Dexter and Horst Buckholz. These seven hired gunmen protect a Mexican village from the bandit Calvera played by Eli Wallach. The film was an Americanization of the Japanese film *The Seven Samurai*. The film implies that you don't need an army to win the war, just seven top "gun men."

The Magnificent Seven of Lean Six Sigma

Over the years, in project after project, I have found myself returning to the same Magnificent Seven Tools of Lean Six Sigma to clean up problems with delay, defects and deviation: process maps, PivotTables, control charts, pareto charts, histograms, fishbones and matrix diagrams.

To Reduce Delays Use These Tools

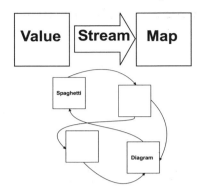

Value Stream Maps identify and remove *unnecessary delays* in any process.

Spaghetti Diagrams identify and eliminate *unnecessary movement* of people or materials.

To Reduce Defects Use These Tools

Less than 4% of any business (one step out of 25) causes over 50% of the defects, deviation and lost profit. I call this **The 4-50 Rule.** Use these tools to find and fix the 4% causing your problems:

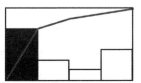

	A	B	C
1	Date	Line	Defect
2	1/2/2010	Line 2	Bent/Damaged flaps
3	1/2/2010	Line 2	Carton will not open
4	1/2/2010	Line 3	Folded flaps
5	1/2/2010	Line 3	Folded flaps
6	1/2/2010	Line 3	Off color
7	1/2/2010	Line 1	Bent/Damaged flaps

Pivot Tables in Excel summarize rows of defect data into numbers that can be graphed. Every million dollar improvement project I've ever worked on started with a Pivot Table.

Control Charts measure and monitor the *error rate* of any process.

Pareto Charts identify the most common type of defect or error. (The 4-50 Rule)

http://www.youtube.com/playlist?list=PL22107B4D01E3AF0B

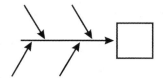

Ishikawa Diagrams document the root causes of each "big bar" on the Pareto chart.

Action Plans organize and prioritize corrective actions.

To Reduce Deviation Use These Tools

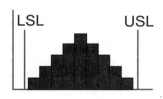

Control Charts measure and monitor the *variability* of any process.

Histograms evaluate deviation from target in process performance.

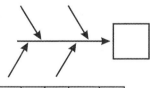

Ishikawa Diagrams show the root causes of defects and deviation.

Action plans organize and schedule corrective actions.

Use This Tool to Collect Data Quickly

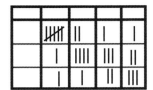

Checksheets are matrix diagrams that can be used to collect data quickly and manually.

To learn more about how to use these tools go to: www.lssmb.com.

Perfect!

When you reduce or eliminate defects and deviation using these tools, your product or service takes a giant leap toward *perfection*. And you don't have to fix everything, just the 4% causing over half of the problems.

I have found that teams equipped with these seven tools can solve most of the problems facing a typical business. Sure, they will need more exotic tools to solve the last one percent of problems, but they won't need them for awhile. And when they do, they will need to look them up anyway.

Are you stuck trying to figure out which Lean Six Sigma tools to use in what order? Master the Magnificent Seven to deliver breakthrough improvements. You'll be surprised how far you can go.

Chapter 5

Implementing Lean Six Sigma

Do You Make These Lean Six Sigma Mistakes?

- Think you have to have CEO involvement to get started?

- Think Lean Six Sigma only works in manufacturing, not services, healthcare, IT, food, and backroom functions like ordering, invoicing, purchasing, payments, etc.?

- Think you need expensive multi-week training to get started?

- Think training leads to results?

- Think it takes months if not years to start getting results?

- Measure success by the number of belts certified and teams started?

- Use Lean Six Sigma to justify your intuitive gut-feel, knee-jerk "solutions" without adequate analysis?

- Start teams without a laser-focused problem to solve?

- Let teams "brainstorm" and select their own problems to solve?

- Try to fix everything simultaneously?

Let's face it, nobody wants Lean Six Sigma. Companies want the bottom-line, profit-enhancing results they think Lean Six Sigma will deliver. And they want it without all of the excessive costs in time and money normally associated with it.

Recession Refocuses Lean Six Sigma

The recent recession has made every company more focused on reducing costs and boosting profits, doing more with less. Since Lean Six Sigma can achieve these benefits, more companies have become interested in Lean Six Sigma, but they want to maximize results while minimizing the risks and costs.

Companies are asking: "Isn't there a better way to implement Lean Six Sigma?" The 10-to-20 day "belt" certifications that span several months are too expensive and slow for most companies recovering from the recession. I say: "Companies don't need lots of training and belts; they need 'Money Belts' who can find ways to save time and money and add those savings to the bottom line." To make it easier for employees and companies to deploy Lean Six Sigma without the high costs, I've put up a complete, no-cost, 8-hour Money Belt video training at www.lssmb.com.

Companies are asking: "How soon can I get results?" Most Six Sigma folklore suggests it will take months or years. I say: "You can do it in five days or less." I have helped teams solve million-dollar problems in anywhere from a few hours to a few days using Lean Six Sigma Demystified.

Companies are asking: "Do I really need Green Belts and Black Belts?" Companies are turning away from certifying "belts." Healthcare companies are training "improvement advisors" rather than certifying belts because **adding certifications to an employee's resume leads to turnover, not improvement**. Since the recession, companies would rather hire Six Sigma expertise than spend time training existing employees.

Companies are asking: "Why is Lean Six Sigma software so expensive?" Companies are balking at buying expensive Six Sigma software. Six Sigma trainers across America have been using the QI Macros because their clients are asking for more affordable Six Sigma software that works in Excel. The QI Macros are an easy-to-use Excel add-in that will do all of the math, graphs and statistics for Six Sigma. Companies can buy 10 copies of the QI Macros for the price of a one copy of most other Six Sigma software packages.

Why is it so affordable? Because Excel does the heavy lifting of drawing charts and diagrams, and managing the data.

Employees are asking: Do I have to learn a lot of math and statistics?" Employees balk at learning Six Sigma formulas and statistics. I say: "You don't need to know electrical engineering to turn on a light switch. So, you don't need to be a statistician to do Six Sigma. Drawing charts and graphs is as easy as clicking your mouse." Your software should know statistics, not your people.

Because of the volume of work and overwhelm that many employees feel, they are saying: "Don't make me think!" Some managers might think this is an silly request, but I think it's a great one. That's why the QI Macros have four powerful "wizards" that demystify data analysis, statistics and charts.

You Don't Need to be a Statistician

A Black Belt on a manufacturing floor may be the one person out of 100 that needs to know statistics, but they don't really need to know statistics. Their Six Sigma software should know statistics. They just need to know when to use a statistic.

Based on our QI Macros customers, even the biggest companies only train about 250 Green Belts and 5 Black Belts a year.

This leaves thousands of employees in the dark about Lean Six Sigma. No wonder it takes forever to implement Lean Six Sigma and it often fails. No wonder it's so slow to catch on.

Again, the Magnificent Seven tools—process maps, PivotTables, control charts, pareto charts, histograms, fishbone and matrix diagrams—will solve most quality problems, especially in service industries. Teaching participants anything else is "overproduction." Training too many belts is overproduction. Companies need "Money Belts" who can find ways to save time and money.

Stop Waiting for Perfect Data

Too many teams get hung up on having "perfect" data. Get over it. There's no such thing as perfect data. All data is systematically distorted to make someone look good during their annual review. The good news is that the data is systematically distorted, so we can use it to make improvements. I've never seen "bad" or "invalid" data. Some data is just more useful than others.

We have to stop kowtowing to managers who say the data's not valid or we need to get better data or do more analysis. I say that if they've got better data, bring it or shut up. Recently, Donald Wheeler said in a Quality Digest interview that "the best analysis is always the simplest analysis that produces the needed insight." Anything else is overkill.

Stop Waiting for Training

Frankly, most Lean Six Sigma training is overkill. The amount of time spent on most projects is waste. Projects can be done in days, not weeks or months. Skill can be acquired in a day, not months or years, at www.lssmb.com.

Lean Six Sigma needs to drink its own Kool-Aid and slash cycle time, defects and deviation to achieve results faster than most people believe is possible.

What's Wrong With Lean Six Sigma?

A Quality Digest survey explored the problems with Six Sigma. What did they discover?

1. Small companies aren't pursuing Six Sigma. Why not? It costs too much using the traditional Six Sigma approach. It can cost $250,000 to train a black belt and bring them up to speed.

2. Companies pursuing Six Sigma seem to abandon it after two or three years. Why? One reason might be that the average life-span of CEOs is only 2-3 years. When leadership changes, Six Sigma vanishes. Most companies are still using the traditional but flawed top-down, all-or-nothing strategy for implementation. Over 50 years of research into how companies and cultures adopt changes like Six Sigma suggests that "to accelerate adoption, REDUCE the number of people involved." Fewer people, faster implementation!

3. Six Sigma is under performing the media hype:

- Only 64% of respondents agreed that Six Sigma had significantly improved profitability.

- Only 50% agreed that Six Sigma had improved customer satisfaction.

- Only 43% agreed that Six Sigma had improved job satisfaction among employees.

OUCH! This means that current approaches to implementing Six Sigma are delivering a paltry 2-sigma performance (30% failure). No wonder so many companies abandon Six Sigma. The companies that are getting results are doing something different. What is it?

4. You don't need Black Belts to get results

80% of respondents agreed that you should use whatever tools are necessary to get the job done. But, when asked which methods and tools yielded the greatest results, survey respondents answered:

- 87% cause-effect analysis (control chart, pareto chart, histogram and fishbone)

- 35% process mapping (value stream mapping and spaghetti diagramming)

- 26% Lean manufacturing

- 20% Statistical process control (SPC—control charts and histograms).

Why is SPC so low? If you improve, but don't implement a control system to sustain the improvement, you'll be right back where you started in a matter of months. This is a common failure.

Top Five Ways Companies Waste Money on Lean Six Sigma

Here's my top five ways companies waste money on Lean Six Sigma. You may not agree with all of them, but don't let that stop you. Hear me out and see if you don't come to a similar conclusion when you see how all of the parts fit together.

1. Getting **Top Level (CEO) commitment** sounds good, but it leads to the next four ways that companies waste money on Lean Six Sigma. There's a lot of folklore about how to implement Lean Six Sigma, none of which is based on science.

   Over 50 years of research into how cultures adopt, adapt and reject change (*Diffusion of Innovations*) suggests that starting with top level commitment invokes the "Stalinist Paradox" which means that you only have a 50/50 chance of success. This is less than a 1-sigma performance. It's no wonder so many Lean Six Sigma efforts fail after only three years.

   And starting at the top just stirs up the corporate immune system—the people who would rather kill a new idea than give it a try.

2. Top down, CEO-driven implementation leads to the "bigger is better", **wall-to-wall, floor-to-ceiling implementation** which sounds like a good thing, but actually invokes the dark side of Pareto's Rule: 80% of the Lean Six Sigma effort only produces 20% of the results. This dilutes results which leads to its cancellation.

3. CEO-led, "Bigger is better" implementations lead to **5-to-20 day trainings** designed for one percent of employees working on a manufacturing factory floor.

   • This kind of training is overkill for the other 99% of employees. If there's anything I've learned over 20 years it's this: the Magnificent Seven methods and tools will solve 99% of the problems.

- From a Lean point of view, long trainings that cover every aspect of Lean Six Sigma are *overproduction*. When training covers too much, employees don't know where to start. And when they don't know where to start, they fail to start at all!

- To reduce costs, companies sometimes train Black Belts to train Green Belts. Trust me, if you've been trained, but haven't done a successful improvement project, you have no business teaching Lean Six Sigma. Success isn't measured in belts, it's measured in bucks.

4. This wall-to-wall, floor-to-ceiling implementation causes **a failure to focus on the three silent killers or productivity and profitability**: delay, defects and deviation that devour a third of total revenue. Leaders often let Lean Six Sigma flounder by:

- Letting teams choose their own problem to solve. Teams invariably want to blame and then fix someone else—customers, suppliers, managers or subordinates.

- Forming teams before you know what problem you're trying to solve. Until you've done the data analysis, you have no idea who should be on the team.

- Trying to use Lean Six Sigma to solve problems it can't solve like employee morale or customer perceptions. These are *effects* of delays, defects and deviation. You can't fix them directly.

- Software – Oddly enough, software is the one place that companies try to scrimp on Six Sigma. You need software to draw all of the improvement charts and diagrams, and control charts to monitor and sustain improvement. Consultants often teach Minitab or JMP because it adds 2-4 days to the training schedule. Minitab is great for consultant revenue and statisticians, but:

  - It's overkill for everyone else.

  - It's expensive which limits the number of licenses available.

  - It requires four days of training (longer training = more consultant revenue).

  - It's a stand-alone program designed by statistics professors for minicomputers, not point-and-click PC users.

Drinking the Lean Six Sigma Kool-Aid

Years ago, when I first got started with Total Quality Management (TQM) we used a top-down, CEO-driven, all-or-nothing approach to implementing TQM, just like companies are doing with Six Sigma. Following the guidance of our consultants, we started and trained hundreds of teams that met for one hour a week. Two years later only a handful of teams had successfully solved a key business problem. Most were mired in the early steps of the problem solving process.

So I decided to try something radical: I applied Six Sigma to itself. I looked at:

- Each stuck team as a "defect."

- The "delays" built into process: the delays between training and application and the delays between team meetings.

I researched and found better methods for doing just about everything involved in implementation.

1. Using one-day, just-in-time (JIT) training, I was able to close the gap between learning and application.

2. Using one-day root cause teams, I was able to eliminate the delays between team meetings. Solutions that used to take months, now take only hours.

3. Using root cause analysis on team failures, I was able to streamline and simplify the process of focusing the improvement so that we only started teams that could succeed. You see, Six Sigma is a data-driven process. If you don't have data about the problem, Six Sigma just won't work. You don't have to have perfect data; there's no such thing, but you do have to have data that can narrow your focus. If not, you're lost.

4. Using the power of "Diffusion", I was able to weave the methods and tools of Lean Six Sigma into the organization with a minimum involvement of key resources.

The Wrong Way to Implement Lean Six Sigma

The current Lean Six Sigma implementation model offered by consultants discourages this type of thinking. Unfortunately for you, it's just wrong.

Lean Six Sigma has been widely applied in manufacturing, but every business process, large or small, service or manufacturing, suffers from delays, defects and deviation that can be eliminated with Lean Six Sigma.

Training alone cannot produce results. **Only improvement projects produce results.** And, with proper focus, these projects can start delivering results immediately, often in five days or less. And projects instill skills in team members far better than training ever could.

It doesn't matter how many belts are certified or teams started. The only thing that matters at the end of the day is bottom-line, profit-enhancing, productivity-improving results. Half of all Six Sigma implementations fail. Many because they are focused on training, not results.

Too many teams implement a solution and then try to retrofit the data to "prove" their solution. Much better, more powerful improvements come from letting the data help you pinpoint what needs to be fixed and then fixing it.

This method of data mining and analysis focuses improvements on the "vital few" problems. Focus on these and results are assured.

Risk-Free Formula For Success

Everyone points to GE as a leader in Six Sigma, but if you look more closely you'll see that Jack Welch had already created a company that managed and even embraced change. So implementing Six Sigma wasn't as hard as it might be in other organizations.

Many people I talk to in various industries say that they tried process improvement and it left a bad taste in their mouths. So Six Sigma not only has to overcome resistance to change, but also the bad taste left by failed implementations.

A Fool Proof Way to Maximize the Benefits of Lean Six Sigma – Crawl-Walk-Run

The U.S. Army used a Crawl-Walk-Run approach to implementing Lean Six Sigma that resulted in a 700:1 return on investment. You can too.

The employee body can make three choices about Lean Six Sigma or any change: adopt, adapt, or reject. In a world of too much to do and too little time, rejection is often the first impulse. People rarely adopt methods completely, so there must be room for adaptation to fit the corporate environment. There are five factors that affect the speed and success of Lean Six Sigma adoption:

1. Trialability-How easy is it to "test drive" Lean Six Sigma?

2. Simplicity-How difficult is it to understand? (Simplify!)

3. Relative benefit-What does it offer over and above what I'm already doing? (How is it better than trial-and-error?)

4. Compatibility-How well does it match our environment?

5. Observability-How easy is it for leaders and opinion makers to see the benefit?

You can also speed up adoption by letting the employees decide for themselves to adopt Six Sigma rather than having the CEO decide for them (although this is how we keep preaching success—get the CEO to commit to widespread change). So, to maximize your chance of success and minimize your initial investment:

1. Use a crawl-walk-run implementation to maximize your success by leveraging the power of the Diffusion of Innovations.

2. Get results as you go:

   – Use data to laser-focus teams on solving mission- and profit-critical problems.

   – Use Just-In-Time training combined with improvement projects to achieve organizational learning.

   – Allow word of mouth from internal "sneezers" to spread the "gospel" of Lean Six Sigma.

3. Start small. Use the 4-50 rule to solve key problems. Remember that less than 4% of any business creates over half the waste and rework. So you don't have to involve more than 4% of your employees or spend a lot of money on widespread training to get results. This means that to accelerate adoption, *reduce the number of people involved*. Get an external Lean Six Sigma consultant to help you find and create solutions using the tools and methods of Six Sigma. Your employees will learn through experience which is far more valuable than classroom training.

– When 4% of organization adopts, Lean Six Sigma sticks.

– When 20% of the organization adopts, it will spread like wildfire.

4. Laser focus to pinpoint problems and maximize results:

– Use data to focus (the 4-50 rule), then, and only then, choose the team.

– Reduce delays, defects and deviation to increase productivity, profits and growth.

- Use SWAT teams to solve problems quickly.

5. Set BHAGs (Big Hairy Audacious Goals) to achieve a 50% reductions in delay, defects and deviation in six months. When you're just starting out, big reductions are often easier to get than you might think, so why not go for them? Setting BHAGs tells teams that this isn't incremental improvement; it's breakthrough improvement.

6. Fly under the radar. Most companies broadcast their Lean Six Sigma initiative, and employees think: "Here comes another one." This usually stirs up the laggards and skeptics—what I call the corporate "immune system." You are much better off to make initial teams successful and let "word of mouth" spread through informal networks, because this is the fastest way for cultures to adopt change.

7. Create initial success. Only start teams that can succeed. Make a small group of early adopters successful. Then another, then another. When the pioneers (early adopters) become successful, they will tell their friends. The pioneers will convince the early settlers who will eventually convince the late settlers. No one will ever convince the laggards and skeptics; they have to convince themselves.

8. Fight the urge to widen your focus; remember the dark side of the 80/20 rule: 80% of your effort will only produce 20% of the benefit.

9. Review and refocus. Once you solve the initial 4% of your core problems, start on the next 4%, then the next. Diffusion research has shown that somewhere between 16-25% involvement will create a "critical mass" that will cause the change to sweep through the culture.

Good News about Productivity and Profitability

When you focus on the 4% that creates over half the waste and rework, your initial teams get big benefits: 50% reduction in defects, waste, and rework and big improvements in the bottom line. By the time you've worked your way through the first 16-20% of your problems, you will get 80% (the 80/20 rule) of the benefits of Lean Six Sigma. And you'll have minimized your costs of implementation. Now you can grow skilled internal Black Belts from your initial improvement team members.

Using a Diffusion of Innovations approach to crawl-walk-run toward Lean Six Sigma implementation will reduce the risk of failure. Using the 3-57 and 4-50 Rules to laser-focus the initial improvement teams will maximize results and accelerate adoption of Lean Six Sigma.

Lean Six Sigma payoffs are huge, but you may want to consider using the power of diffusion to ensure that the methods and tools take root in your business and flourish. But it's up to you. You can choose the conventional wisdom which gives you only a 50-50 chance at success or choose the power of diffusion which increases your odds substantially.

The corporate jury is still out on Six Sigma. Without dramatic examples of success, Lean Six Sigma will go the way of TQM and quality circles. I encourage you to be a Lean Six Sigma Money Belt. Show me the money! Develop a rich resume of successful projects that give meaning to your skills. Tell your leadership, your customers, and the world how much you've saved.

It's up to you. Will you follow the path offered by the merchants of Lean Six Sigma Folklore or use the science of Diffusion to maximize your chances of success? Haven't you waited long enough to start plugging the leaks in your cash flow?

Be a Money Belt!

Chapter 6

Wrangling Lean Six Sigma Teams

I have found that every successful team has three main players: dreamers, realists, and critics (a.k.a. devil's advocates). Dreamers can easily imagine possible improvements. Realists turn these dreams into reality. Dreamers and Realists are both motivated to *move toward possibilities* without necessarily considering the liabilities. Critics are "problem solvers." They can look at the dreams, plans, and realities, and tell you what's missing or in error. This is the great value of the critic-they keep you out of the inevitable tar pits.

If your team doesn't have at least one dreamer, one realist and one critic, your team will struggle to first solve the problem, then come up with viable solutions and an implementation plan.

Unfortunately, critics aren't very good at communicating their issues and objections. Instead of asking questions that the dreamer and realist can answer, they make statements about possible problems like:

"We wouldn't want to have the same kind of problem we had on our last project."

And they'll keep repeating the same statement in the hopes that everyone else will see the glaring error that they see. This grates on the dreamers and realists because they want to move forward, but the critic won't let the team move forward until their objection is "heard."

When the dreamers and realists hear this kind of statement, they think "Of course we wouldn't want that; what's your question?" And that is the heart of the communication difficulty: dreamers and realists can answer questions about the dream, plan and reality, but they don't know what to do with a *statement* about possible tar pits.

So if you have a critic on your team, consider learning how to turn their statements into "how" questions that the dreamer and realist can answer:

"So are you asking: *how* we can avoid the kind of problem we had last year?"

Get the idea? And if you are the critic on your team, consider shifting what seems like a perfectly logical statement into a question that the dreamers and realists can answer. They will love you for it and stop hating you.

Celebrate your devil's advocates. They will keep you out of hot water and help make you more successful than you've ever dreamed. All you have to do is translate their statements into powerful "how" questions that your dreamers and realists can understand.

To learn more about how to deal with difficult people go to: www.qimacros.com/knowwareezines/201003-dealing-with-difficult-people-p2.html.

Chapter 7

Do Your Employees Have the Tools They Need to Succeed at Lean Six Sigma?

Consider the surprisingly high cost of Lean Six Sigma:

- $250,000 to train a Six Sigma Black Belt and get them up to speed.
- $60,000 to train a Six Sigma Green Belt.

With the high cost of training a Six Sigma belt, you'd think companies would do whatever it takes to make their belts productive. More often, however, IT and purchasing get involved and scrimp on the software needed to be successful at Six Sigma.

Most companies will spring for a few shared copies of Minitab or JMP, but is that where your data resides? No, your data is in Microsoft Excel.

To make your belts productive, isn't that where your Six Sigma tools should be?

And after your belts have helped a team Define, Measure, Analyze and Improve a process, someone has to implement a Control system to monitor the improved process. Once you rise above a 3-sigma performance, you will need control charts to monitor the process, because you can no longer detect process changes with your five senses.

After a process has been improved, your Money Belts should move on to other problems. Who "controls" the improved process? I call them No Belts—the employees who work the process. Those employees will need control charts that are easy to use and update.

You won't want to spend $2,500 a copy to equip these employees with software, nor will you want to spend thousands more training them to use it. You will want control chart software that's more affordable and easy to learn.

Solution: The QI Macros are an affordable Six Sigma software add-in for Microsoft Excel. They work right in Excel to create control charts, histograms and Pareto charts easily. There are over 90 fill-in-the-blank templates for everything from control charts to flow charts. It will make your Black Belts, Green Belts and No Belts more productive.

I sponsored a debate at our Cincinnati Six Sigma User's Group. 100% of those who chose to speak all agreed that 90% of all projects need nothing more sophisticated than the nice and easy, no training required, QI Macros authored by Jay Arthur and updated quarterly for a modest fee.

Daryl N. Zeigler, MD, MMM, CPE, CSSBB

Theory of Constraints – An improvement methodology known as the Theory of Constraints suggests that four main constraints hold a company back: resources, market, policy and dummy constraints.

Information Technologies (IT) has policy constraints: Select a single, stand-alone software package for each application.

Purchasing has policy and resource constraints: Minimize the cost of each item purchased. When stand-alone software costs $2,500 per copy, purchasing and IT try to restrict access and total cost.

Dummy Constraints – Sadly, policy and resource constraints are both Dummy Constraints—constraints that can be easily remedied with a little money. The QI Macros only cost a couple hundred bucks. Wouldn't you spend $200 to make a $250,000 Black Belt more productive? Wouldn't you spend $200 to make a $60,000 Green Belt more productive? Wouldn't you spend that to equip your No Belts with the software they need to monitor and sustain the improvement so that you don't slip back into marginal levels of performance? With our free video training on-line, they can learn how to use the software without days of classroom training.

I had one office person go to a Greenbelt training class which used Minitab. He came back and couldn't even create a Pareto chart. I showed him how to do it with QI Macros and he learned how to do it in, well, 5 seconds. Tough stuff. - Patient Safety Manager

Biggest Mistake Companies Make With Six Sigma: Failure to equip your No Belts with control chart software to control the process means that in a short period of time performance will slip back to its original, 3-sigma level. All that time and money you spent on Black

Belt training, team meetings and implementing the improvement will be lost.

Do your employees have the tools they need to maximize the benefits of Lean Six Sigma? Probably not.

The QI Macros are an affordable, powerful, easy-to-use solution to your dummy software constraints. Haven't you waited long enough to maximize the productivity and ROI of your Black Belts, Green Belts and No Belts, or are you going to keep living with the constraints?

Start Today!

- Be a Money Belt! Learn how to apply the Magnificent Seven Tools at www.lssmb.com. There are eight hours of video training with case studies and exercises.

- You will need software to help draw the Magnificent Seven. Download a 90-day trial of the QI Macros at www.qimacros.com/demystified.html.

- When you find you need more personalized help, we offer:

  a. Books: Lean Six Sigma Demystified and Lean Six Sigma for Hospitals

  b. Data analysis and project development

  c. Phone and webinar coaching

  d. Onsite workshops and boot camps to make your teams successful immediately.

Haven't you waited long enough to start systematically plugging the leaks in your cash flow? Isn't it time to stop relying on gut feel and take a step up to the next level of performance? To learn more, go to www.qimacros.com. **Or call: 888-468-1537** (303-756-9144)

Jay Arthur, The KnowWare® Man, works with companies that want to eliminate delay, defects and deviation—the three silent killers of productivity and profitability. Using Jay's approach, one Baby Bell eliminated five of their top order errors, resulting in annual savings of $3,000,000. A hospital group saved $5,000,000 a year in denied charges and reduced turnaround time for appealed claims from 300 days to 45 days. Haven't you waited long enough to start using a proven method for routinely saving millions and boosting your bottom line?

Want to learn more about my bare-bones, quick-and-dirty approach to Lean Six Sigma? Consider my books:

Lean Six Sigma Demystified is filled with examples and case studies about using the Magnificent Seven tools to solve all kinds of problems with delays defects and deviation in record time.

Lean Six Sigma for Hospitals is filled with healthcare examples and case studies about how to get a faster, better, cheaper hospital in five days.

KnowWare International Inc.
2253 S. Oneida St. Ste 3D
Denver, CO 80224
(888) 468-1537
knowwareman@qimacros.com
www.qimacros.com

Bibliography

Anderson, Chris, Free: How Today's Smartest Businesses Profit by Giving Something for Nothing, Hyperion, New York, 2009.

Arthur, Jay, Lean Six Sigma Demystified, McGraw-Hill, NY, 2011.

Arthur, Jay, Lean Six Sigma For Hospitals, McGraw-Hill, NY, 2011.

Barker, Joel, Future Edge, William Morrow, NY, 1992.

Collins, Jim, Good to Great: Why Some Companies Make the Leap... and Others Don't, HarperCollins, NY, 2001.

Dusharme, Dirk. "Six Sigma Survey," Quality Digest, February 2003 and September 2004.

Gladwell, Malcolm. The Tipping Point. Boston: Little Brown, 2002.

Godin, Seth. Unleashing the Ideavirus. New York: Hyperion, 2001.

Levitt, Steven D. and Stephen J. Dubner, Freakonomics: A Rogue Economist Explores the Hidden Side of Everything, New York: HarperCollins, 2005.

Liker, Jeffrey. The Toyota Way. New York: McGraw-Hill, 2004.

Miller, Ken. We Don't Make Widgets—Overcoming the Myths That Keep Government from Radically Improving. New York: Governing Books, 2006.

Rogers, Everett. Diffusion of Innovations, 4th ed. New York: Free Press, 1995.

Stauk, George. and Thomas M. Hout. Competing Against Time. New York: Free Press, 1990

Womack, James P., and Daniel T. Jones. Lean Thinking, New York: Simon & Schuster, 1996.

Yes! I want Jay Arthur's fast, fun and easy-to-use Lean Six Sigma Systems to work for me! *Please send the software and books indicated below. Prices Good Thru 6/30/12*

QI Macros for Excel	Free, Perfect and Now
Item# 230	**Item # 206**
QI Macros For Excel Software	Lean Six Sigma
CD with 36 page User Guide	Money Belt Manifesto
Only $199	**Only $9.95**
Add $8 U.S. S&H	*Add $5 U.S. S&H*
Add $25 for FedEx	*Add $20 for FedEx*

Your Name _____

Company _____

Mailing Address _____

P.O. Box _____   Apt/Ste. _____

City, ST, Zip _____

Phone _____

Fax _____

Email _____

Purchase Order Number _____

☐VISA ☐MasterCard ☐ AMEX

_____ Exp._____

Signature _____

Order and download software on-line at **www.qimacros.com**

Orders-only, Toll-free: (888) 468-1535 or (303) 757-2039

Questions: **888-468-1537** or 303-756-9144

Toll-Free Fax: (888)468-1536 or (303) 756-3107

Mail: KnowWare, 2253 S. Oneida St. Ste 3D
Denver, CO 80224